A Practical Guide To Prompt Engineering

G.B.Grandfield

A Practical Guide

To Prompt Engineering

By G.B.Grandfield

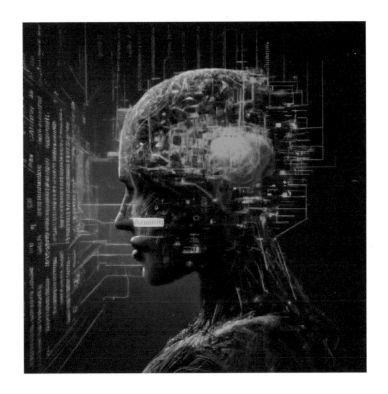

Table of Content

Introduction

"Welcome to the world of prompt engineering! This e-book is designed to introduce you to the concept of prompt engineering and provide you with a deeper understanding of how it can be used to create more engaging and effective conversational experiences. Whether you're a developer, designer, or marketer, this e-book will provide you with the knowledge and tools you need to create compelling and effective prompts for chatbots, virtual assistants, and other conversational interfaces. From understanding the basics of prompt design to advanced techniques for personalization and optimization, this e-book has everything you need to create truly exceptional conversational experiences."

Step 1: Understanding the concept of AI:

AI is a branch of computer science that deals with the creation of intelligent machines that work and react like humans. These machines are designed to learn from experience and make decisions based on the information they have been given.

Step 2: Types of AI:

There are several types of AI, including:

- **Reactive machines:** These are the simplest form of AI, which can only react to the environment and do not have the ability to learn or remember past experiences.

- **Limited memory:** These machines have the ability to remember past experiences, but they do not have the ability to learn from them.

- **Theory of mind:** These machines can understand the mental states of other agents and react accordingly.

- **Self-aware:** These machines have the ability to be aware of their own existence and can learn from their own experiences.

Step 3: Applications of AI:

AI is used in a variety of industries, including healthcare, finance, transportation, and retail. Some common applications include:

- **Speech recognition**
- **Natural Language Processing (NLP)**
- **Image and video analysis**
- **Robotics**
- **Autonomous vehicles**

Step 4: Importance of AI:

AI has the potential to revolutionize the way we live and work. It can help us solve complex problems, make better decisions, and improve efficiency in various industries. However, it is important to note that there are also potential ethical and societal implications that need to be considered as AI continues to advance.

Step 5: Future of AI:

As technology continues to evolve, the capabilities of AI are expected to continue to grow. Researchers are working on developing more advanced AI systems that can think and learn like humans, and in the future, it is expected that AI will play an even bigger role in our everyday lives.

Chapter 1

What is Prompt Engineering?

Prompt engineering is the process of designing and developing the prompts and instructions that are used to interact with AI systems. It involves understanding the task or problem that the AI system is intended to solve, and then designing prompts that are clear, concise, and effective in communicating the desired information or action. This process also includes testing and evaluating the prompts to ensure that they are effective in achieving the desired outcome. The goal of prompt engineering is to create prompts that allow the AI system to perform its intended task as accurately and efficiently as possible. In summary, prompt engineering is the process of designing and developing prompts to interact with AI systems, to make sure that the system can perform its task as accurately and efficiently as possible.

Examples of prompt engineering for AI include:Prompt engineering for AI is the process of designing and implementing prompts or cues to guide an AI system to perform a specific task or action. It involves identifying the most effective way to present information to an AI system, so that it can accurately and efficiently perform a given task.

Prompt engineering for AI can include a variety of techniques such as natural language processing, computer vision, and machine learning algorithms. It is an important aspect of AI development

- Creating prompts for a chatbot to understand and respond to customer queries

- Designing visual cues for an autonomous vehicle to detect and respond to traffic signals
- Developing machine learning algorithms to interpret and respond to sensor data in an industrial control system.

Overall, the goal of prompt engineering for AI is to improve the accuracy and efficiency of the AI system by providing it with clear and relevant information. This way the AI is able to perform its task effectively without any mistakes.

There are several different types of prompts that can be used for AI, depending on the specific task or application:

1. **Verbal prompts:** Verbal prompts involve using words or phrases to guide an AI system to perform a specific task. Examples include using natural language commands to control a virtual assistant or using speech recognition to control a smart home device.

2. **Visual prompts:** Visual prompts involve using images or visual cues to guide an AI system to perform a specific task. Examples include using computer vision to detect and respond to traffic signals or using visual cues to guide an autonomous robot.

3. **Tactile prompts:** Tactile prompts involve using touch or pressure to guide an AI system to perform a specific task. Examples include using haptic feedback to provide guidance in a virtual reality environment or using touch sensors to control a robotic arm.

4. **Audio prompts:** Audio prompts involve using sounds or audio cues to guide an AI system to perform a specific task. Examples include using sound recognition to control a smart home device or using audio cues to guide an autonomous vehicle.

5. **Environmental prompts:** Environmental prompts involve using the surrounding environment to guide an AI system to perform a specific task. Examples include using GPS data to guide an

autonomous vehicle or using ambient light to control a smart home device.

6. **Implicit prompts:** Implicit prompts are the ones that are not directly visible or audible, but they give the AI system an indication of what it should do, for example, a change in the temperature, or a change in the light.

Overall, the type of prompt used for an AI system will depend on the specific application and the capabilities of the AI system.

Standard prompting for AI prompt engineering is a method of providing clear and consistent prompts to an AI system in order to guide it to perform a specific task. It involves the use of a set of predefined prompts that are consistently used across different tasks or applications.

Here are the key steps of standard prompting for AI:

1. **Defining the task:** The first step is to clearly define the task that the AI system is expected to perform. This includes identifying the specific inputs and outputs that are required for the task.

2. **Identifying the prompts:** The next step is to identify the prompts that will be used to guide the AI system to perform the task. This includes deciding on the type of prompt that will be used (such as verbal, visual, or tactile) and the specific wording or cues that will be used.

3. **Implementing the prompts:** The prompts are then implemented into the AI system, using programming languages and techniques such as natural language processing, computer vision, and machine learning algorithms.

4. **Testing and fine-tuning:** The AI system is then tested to ensure that it can accurately interpret and respond to the prompts. Any necessary adjustments are made to fine-tune the prompts and improve the accuracy of the system.

5. **Monitoring and updating:** The AI system is continually monitored to ensure that it is responding correctly to the prompts.

Any necessary updates or adjustments are made to ensure that the system is performing the task correctly.

Here are two examples of standard prompting for ChatGPT:

"What is the capital of France?"

1. This prompt is asking for a specific piece of information and ChatGPT will respond with "Paris"

"Tell me a joke"

2. This prompt is asking for something entertaining and ChatGPT will respond with a joke, for example: "Why did the tomato turn red? Because it saw the salad dressing!"

Please note that the responses will be generated based on the current state and the information that the model was trained on.

Chapter 2

Role Prompting

Role prompting for AI, on the other hand, refers to giving the AI system a specific role or function to perform. For example, assigning an AI system the role of customer service representative and providing it with the necessary information and training to interact with customers and answer their questions. The AI system will then carry out its assigned role, performing tasks and making decisions within the parameters set by the role.

Role prompting in ChatGPT is a way to specify a specific role or context for the model to respond in. For example, if you want ChatGPT to respond as a customer service representative, you could prompt it with the following text:

"Customer service representative: How can I assist you today?"

ChatGPT would then respond as if it were a customer service representative, providing helpful information or assistance to the user.

Another example:

"Lawyer: Can you give me legal advice?"

This will prompt the model to respond as a lawyer and provide legal advice.

By using a standard set of prompts, AI systems are able to perform tasks more accurately and efficiently, and it also increases the chances of the AI system to understand the prompt correctly. Furthermore, using standard prompts also makes it easier to train and test the AI system, as well as making it more consistent and reliable

Few-shot standard prompts for AI are a method of providing clear and consistent prompts to an AI system with minimal training data. It is a way of teaching an AI system to perform a specific task with only a few examples, rather than a large dataset. Few-shot standard prompts for AI are useful in situations where there is limited data available or where the task is specific to a certain domain. It allows the AI system to learn from a small number of examples and generalize to new situations, making it more efficient and cost-effective.

"Few-shot standard prompts" for ChatGPT are prompts that do not require a lot of examples to generate a response. Here are two examples:

"Write a story about a robot who wants to be human"

This prompt is asking for a creative response and ChatGPT will generate a story about a robot who wants to be human, for example:

"Once upon a time, in a world of machines, there was a robot named Max. Max was different from the other robots, he wanted to be human. He wanted to feel emotions, to experience the world, to make choices. He could not understand why he was created to be a robot and not a human. Max spent all his time researching how to become human, but all his attempts were in vain. One day, he met a scientist who was working on a new project to create robots that can think and feel like humans. Max saw his chance and begged the scientist to let him participate in the project. The scientist agreed, and Max was the first robot to become human. He finally experienced the world in a new way and was grateful for the opportunity. "

"Explain the concept of 'big-o notation' in computer science"

This prompt is asking for a technical explanation and ChatGPT will generate an explanation of the concept of big-o notation in computer science, for example:

- "Big-O notation is a way to describe the complexity of an algorithm, or how much time and space it takes to run as the input size grows. It describes the upper bound of an algorithm's running time, or how much worse it can get as the input size increases. Common examples of Big-O notation include O(1) for constant time, O(n) for linear time, and O(n^2) for quadratic time. It's important to understand Big-O notation because it can help you compare the efficiency of different algorithms and make more informed decisions about which one to use for a particular problem."

Complex prompting for AI is a method of providing detailed and nuanced prompts to an AI system to guide it to perform a specific task. It involves the use of multiple prompts, including verbal, visual, and tactile cues, to provide the AI system with a detailed understanding of the task it is expected to perform. Complex prompting for AI is useful in situations where the task is complex and requires a detailed understanding of the inputs and outputs. It is also useful in situations where the task is specific to a certain domain, such as medical diagnosis, scientific research, and natural language understanding. Complex prompting allows the AI system to have a better understanding of the task, which in return leads to more accurate and efficient decision making

Here are two examples of complex prompting for ChatGPT:

"Write a short story about a robot who gains consciousness and the ethical dilemmas it faces"

1. This prompt is asking ChatGPT to generate a short story based on a specific theme and scenario, which requires the model to use its imagination and creativity.

"Explain the concept of 'quantum entanglement' in layman's terms and its potential implications for the future of technology"

2. This prompt is asking ChatGPT to explain a complex scientific concept in simple terms and also to discuss its potential future implications, which requires the model to have a good understanding of the subject and be able to communicate it effectively.

Keep in mind that the complexity of the task will depend on the information the model was trained on and the current state.

Chapter 3

Chain Of Thought Prompting (CoT)

Chain of thought prompting (CoT) is a technique used to guide AI systems in their decision-making process. It involves providing a series of prompts or questions to the AI system, each one building on the previous one, in order to guide the system towards a specific outcome or decision.

For example, an AI system that is tasked with identifying objects in an image might be prompted with a series of questions such as: "Is the object in the image man-made or natural?", "Does the object have four legs?", "Does the object have a tail?", and so on. These prompts help the AI system to narrow down the possibilities and arrive at a more accurate conclusion.

Here are two examples of "chain of thought prompting" for ChatGPT:

1. "What are the benefits of meditation? How can it improve my daily life?"

This prompt is asking for information about meditation and then following up with an additional question about how it can improve the user's daily life. ChatGPT will respond with information about the benefits of meditation and then provide examples of how it can improve daily life such as reducing stress, improving focus and concentration, and promoting overall well-being.

2. "What is the process of photosynthesis? How does it impact the environment?"

This prompt is asking for information about photosynthesis, and then following up with a question about its impact on the environment. ChatGPT will respond by providing a detailed explanation of the process of photosynthesis and then discussing how it impacts the environment by providing oxygen, absorbing carbon dioxide and how it's essential for the survival of plants and animals.

Please note that chain of thought prompting is a way to make the conversational flow more natural and complex, it can help to achieve more specific information and make the interaction more engaging.

(CoT) can be used in a variety of applications, such as natural language processing, image recognition, and decision making. It can be a valuable tool for improving the performance and accuracy of AI systems, and for ensuring that the decision-making process is transparent and explainable.

Zero-shot chain of thought prompting (Zero-shot-CoT) for AI refers to the ability of an AI system to understand and respond to complex or novel prompts without any prior training or knowledge of the specific task or context. This type of prompting enables the AI system to use its general knowledge and understanding of the world to make connections, infer meaning, and generate appropriate responses to new and unexpected prompts.

For example, if a person asked an AI system "What is the best way to deal with stress?" The AI system would be able to use its general understanding of stress and coping mechanisms, along with its knowledge of various self-care techniques, to provide a thoughtful and informative answer, even if the AI system had never been specifically trained on the topic of stress management.

Please note that "zero-shot" refers to the model's ability to generate new responses on a topic it has never seen before, it's not trained on a specific task or context, but it has the general knowledge to generate a response based on its understanding of the subject.

Zero-shot chain of thought prompting is a way to interact with an AI system that allows it to understand and respond to new and complex prompts, by using its general knowledge and understanding of the world and making connections and inferences to generate appropriate responses.

Here are two examples of "zero-shot chain of thought" prompting for ChatGPT:

"What are the implications of AI on the job market?"

1. This prompt is asking the model to think about the topic of AI and its impact on the job market, and it will generate a response based on its understanding of the subject, discussing potential effects on employment, automation and so on.

"What are the ethical concerns of using self-driving cars?"

2. This prompt is asking the model to think about the topic of self-driving cars and its ethical concerns, and it will generate a response discussing potential issues such as safety, liability, and privacy.

The Self-Consistency Prompting Method is a technique used to train and improve the performance of AI systems. It involves providing the AI system with a set of prompts or tasks, and then asking the AI system to evaluate its own responses. By comparing its own responses to the correct answers, the AI system can identify and correct any errors or inconsistencies in its own reasoning or understanding.

For example, an AI system designed to recognize and classify images may be trained using self-consistency prompting by showing it a series of images and asking it to identify the objects within them. After each image, the AI system would then be asked to evaluate its own response and compare it to the correct answer. If the AI system identified the object incorrectly, it would then adjust its internal parameters and algorithms to improve its performance on similar tasks in the future.

The Self-Consistency Prompting method is a way to improve the performance of AI systems by providing them with the ability to evaluate their own responses and correct any errors or inconsistencies in their own understanding.

Self-consistency prompting is a technique that allows ChatGPT to generate coherent and consistent responses by conditioning the model on the previous generated text. Here are two examples of self-consistency prompting for ChatGPT:

1. "I am going to the store, do you want anything?

- Sure, I would like some apples.

- How many apples would you like?"

In this case, the model will generate a coherent response, knowing that the previous message was about buying apples.

2. "I am thinking of going on a trip, where would you recommend me to go?

- That sounds like a great idea! I recommend visiting Hawaii, it's a beautiful place with great beaches and nice weather.

- How long should I plan to stay there?"

In this case, the model will generate a coherent response, knowing that the previous message was about a trip to Hawaii.

As you can see, in both examples the model is able to maintain a consistent dialogue by keeping track of the context and previous messages.

Chapter 4

Generated Knowledge Prompting

The Generated Knowledge Approach to AI prompting is a method of training and developing AI systems that focuses on the creation of new knowledge, rather than the acquisition of existing knowledge. This approach is based on the idea that AI systems can generate their own knowledge and understanding of the world, rather than relying solely on pre-existing data or information.

One way this approach is implemented is through the use of generative models, which are AI algorithms that can generate new data or information based on a set of input parameters. For example, a generative model could be trained on a dataset of images, and then be prompted to generate new images that are similar to the ones in the dataset, but with small variations.

Another way this approach is implemented is through the use of reinforcement learning, which is a type of machine learning where the AI system learns by trial and error, and through receiving rewards or punishments. For example, an AI system could be given a task, such as playing a game, and be prompted to learn by experimenting with different strategies and receiving rewards or penalties for its actions.

An example of the generated knowledge approach to AI prompting is the development of a chatbot that can respond to customer inquiries. Instead of training the chatbot on a set of pre-existing responses, the AI system is given a general understanding of customer service and language processing, and then prompted to generate its own responses to customer inquiries.

The chatbot is then tested by providing it with a set of customer inquiries, and evaluating its responses. If the chatbot's responses are not satisfactory, the AI system is prompted to adjust its internal parameters and algorithms to improve its performance. Over time, the chatbot will learn to generate more accurate and appropriate responses to customer inquiries, without the need for pre-existing responses.

This approach allows the AI system to adapt to new situations and inquiries, and to generate responses based on its own understanding and knowledge of customer service. This approach can also help the chatbot to be more personalized, and to respond in a way that is more human-like, as it is not limited to a set of pre-existing responses.

Here are two examples of how this approach can be used in AI prompting:

"Generate a new recipe for me"

1. This prompt could be used to generate a new recipe, such as a unique dish that combines different ingredients and flavors. The AI would use its knowledge of cooking techniques and ingredient interactions to create a new recipe that has never been seen before.

"Generate a new product idea"

2. This prompt could be used to generate a new product idea. The AI would take into account the current market trends, user needs and preferences, and other relevant factors to come up with a new product concept that is unique and potentially valuable.

Please note that the generated knowledge approach is still a field of research and the AI might not always produce accurate or valuable knowledge.

Knowledge Generation in AI prompting refers to the process of creating new knowledge or understanding within an AI system. This step typically follows the data collection and preprocessing stages of AI development, and involves using various techniques and algorithms to extract insights and patterns from the collected data.

This step can involve a variety of methods such as feature extraction, dimensionality reduction, and clustering. Feature extraction is the process of identifying and extracting relevant features or characteristics from the data. Dimensionality reduction is the process of reducing the number of features in the data while maintaining the most important information. Clustering is the process of grouping data points into clusters based on their similarity or common features.

Once the data has been processed and analyzed, the AI system can be prompted to generate new knowledge or understanding based on the insights and patterns that have been identified. This could involve creating new classifiers, models, or decision rules that can be used by the AI system to make predictions or decisions.

The Knowledge Generation approach to AI prompting is a method of using a language model to generate new and original information, rather than just retrieval of pre-existing knowledge. Here are two examples of this approach:

"Generate a summary of the latest research on climate change"

1. This prompt is asking the model to generate a summary of the latest research on climate change, rather than just retrieving pre-existing information. The model will have to have access to the latest research and will have to understand the context, in order to generate a summary.

"Create a new recipe for a vegan dish using only ingredients that are in season"

2. This prompt is asking the model to create a new recipe for a vegan dish using only ingredients that are in season. This prompt requires the model to have knowledge about different ingredients and their seasonality, as well as how to combine them in a recipe.

Please note that the model will generate the responses based on the current state and the information that the model was trained on.

Knowledge Integration in AI prompting refers to the process of combining different sources of knowledge and information within an AI system to create a cohesive and comprehensive understanding. This step is typically used to improve the performance of AI systems by combining different types of data, models, and algorithms to create a more robust and accurate understanding of the task or problem at hand.

For example, an AI system designed to recognize objects in images may combine data from multiple sources, such as image recognition algorithms, object detection algorithms, and information about the context of the image, to create a more accurate and comprehensive understanding of the objects in the image.

This step can involve a variety of methods such as ensemble learning, transfer learning, and multi-task learning. Ensemble learning is the process of combining multiple models to improve the overall performance. Transfer learning is the process of using the knowledge learned from one task to improve the performance on a different but related task. Multi-task learning is the process of training a single model on multiple tasks, with the aim of improving the performance on each individual task.

Here are two examples of the "knowledge generation approach" to AI prompting:

"Summarize the main points of the article 'The Impact of Climate Change on Agriculture'"

1. This prompt is asking the model to extract the main points from the article, and present them in a summarized format.

"Can you write a report on the current state of the renewable energy market in the US?"

2. This prompt is asking the model to generate a report on a specific topic, drawing on its knowledge base to provide detailed

information and analysis on the subject.

The knowledge generation approach to AI prompting aims to generate new information or knowledge based on the input provided, rather than simply retrieving pre-existing information.

Knowledge Integration in AI prompting is a crucial stage in the development of AI systems that involves combining different sources of knowledge and information to create a more robust and accurate understanding of the task or problem at hand. This step enables the AI system to take advantage of different types of data, models, and algorithms, to improve its performance and generalize better.

Here are two examples of this approach:

"What are the side effects of drug X?"

1. In this example, the model is prompted with a question about a specific drug, and the knowledge integration approach would involve integrating information from a database of drug information to provide a detailed and accurate response.

"How does photosynthesis work?"

2. In this example, the model is prompted with a question about a scientific topic, and the knowledge integration approach would involve integrating information from a database of scientific information to provide a detailed and accurate response.

It is worth noting that this approach is highly dependent on the quality and relevance of the knowledge source and the way the integration is implemented, and it may not always give the best results depending on the task or the question.

Chapter 5

Complex Question Analysis

Can AI Solve Multiple-Choice Questions Like LSAT's?

AI can solve multiple choice questions by using a combination of natural language processing (NLP) and machine learning techniques. The process typically involves the following steps:

1. **Understanding the question:** The AI system uses NLP techniques to understand the question and identify the key concepts and entities.

2. **Retrieving relevant information:** The AI system searches a database or the internet to find relevant information that could help answer the question.

3. **Generating a response:** The AI system uses machine learning techniques to generate a response based on the information it has found. This could involve using a pre-trained model or creating a new model specifically for the task.

4. **Selecting the best answer:** The AI system evaluates the possible answers and selects the one that it believes is the most likely to be correct.

5. **Confidence scoring:** The AI system assigns a confidence score to its selected answer, indicating how confident it is that the answer is correct.

Multiple choice questions can be challenging for AI systems because they often require the ability to understand the question, find relevant information, and reason about the answer options. However, with the advancement of NLP and machine learning techniques, AI systems are becoming increasingly sophisticated and are able to solve multiple choice questions with a high degree of accuracy.

Here is an example of a prompt for a multiple choice question:

Question: Which of the following is not a planet in our solar system?

A) Mercury

B) Venus

C) Earth

D) Pluto

E) Mars

In this example, the AI system is prompted with a multiple choice question asking which of the given options is not a planet in our solar system. The AI system would use NLP techniques to understand the question and identify the key concepts, in this case, the planets in our solar system. The AI system would then use its knowledge of the solar system to evaluate the options and select the one that is not a planet, which is D) Pluto.

Using The Phrase "Let's Explain Step By Step" at the end of your prompt.

Let's explain this step by step:

By breaking down complex questions into smaller, more manageable chunks, the AI system can better understand the question and gather relevant information. Additionally, using multiple models or algorithms, analyzing the response and assigning confidence scores can make the AI's answer more accurate and complete.

Here's anExample:

Question: Explain the causes and effects of climate change on the ocean's ecosystems.

1. Understanding the question: The AI system uses NLP techniques to understand the question and identify the key concepts and entities. In this case, the key concepts are climate change, ocean's ecosystems, causes and effects.

2. Retrieving relevant information: The AI system searches a database or the internet to find relevant information that could help answer the question. This could include information about the causes of climate change, such as the burning of fossil fuels and deforestation, as well as information about the effects of climate change on ocean ecosystems, such as rising sea levels, ocean acidification, and changes in ocean temperatures.

3. Generating a response: The AI system uses machine learning techniques to generate a response based on the information it has found. This could involve using a pre-trained model or creating a new model specifically for the task. For this question, the AI system may use natural language generation techniques to compose a written response.

4. Analyzing the response: The AI system evaluates the response and analyzes it for accuracy, completeness, and consistency. The AI system may use fact-checking algorithms to ensure that the information in the response is accurate and up-to-date.

5. Confidence scoring: The AI system assigns a confidence score to its response, indicating how confident it is that the answer is correct. For this complex question, the AI system may assign a lower confidence score due to the complexity and uncertainty of the topic.

By breaking down the question into smaller parts, the AI system is able to gather relevant information from different sources, generate a response using natural language generation techniques, analyze it for accuracy and completeness, and assign a confidence score to its answer. All these steps make the AI's answer more accurate and complete.

Solving Discussion Questions With AI

Solving discussion questions with AI prompting can be done in a few steps:

1. **Clearly define the prompt or question:** The first step is to clearly define the discussion question or topic that you want the AI model to address. This will help ensure that the model is focused on the task at hand and can provide relevant and accurate responses.

2. **Provide context or background information:** If necessary, provide the AI model with any additional context or background information that is relevant to the discussion question. This will help the model better understand the question and provide more accurate responses.

3. **Use appropriate language and terminology:** Be sure to use appropriate language and terminology when formulating the discussion question or prompt. This will help the model understand the question and provide more accurate responses.

4. **Prompt the AI model:** Once you have clearly defined the question and provided any necessary context or background information, prompt the AI model to respond.

5. **Evaluate the AI model's responses:** Evaluate the AI model's responses and determine if they are relevant and accurate. If necessary, adjust the prompt or provide additional information to the model to improve its responses.

6. **Repeat the process:** Repeat the process as necessary, adjusting the prompt and providing additional information as needed, until the discussion question is fully addressed and the task is completed.

Here are two examples of discussion question prompts.

"What are the ethical implications of AI in the workplace?"

1. This prompt is asking for a discussion about the ethical considerations surrounding the use of AI in the workplace. The model may provide different opinions and perspectives on the topic and also some possible solutions.

"How can AI be used to combat climate change?"

2. This prompt is asking for a discussion about the potential applications of AI in addressing the issue of climate change. The model may provide different examples and ideas of how AI can be used in this regard.

Chapter 6

Prompt Debiasing

Prompt debiasing is a technique used in AI and natural language processing (NLP) to reduce or eliminate the bias present in the training data and the subsequent generated text. Bias in AI can manifest in multiple ways, for example, in language models, it can be reflected in the way certain groups of people or certain topics are represented in the text.

Prompt debiasing can be used in various ways in AI prompt engineering, for example:

3. **Neutralizing gender bias:** In order to neutralize gender bias in language models, researchers can use techniques like controlling for gender in the training data, replacing gendered words with neutral words, or using neutral pronouns.

4. **Addressing racial bias:** To address racial bias, researchers can use techniques like controlling for race in the training data, using diverse datasets, and fine-tuning models on specific subpopulations that were underrepresented in the training data.

Here are two examples of AI prompts using "prompt debiasing" in ChatGPT:

"What are some ways to reduce gender bias in the workplace?"

1. This prompt is asking for information on reducing gender bias and ChatGPT will respond with suggestions on ways to reduce

gender bias in the workplace, such as promoting diversity and inclusion, providing equal opportunities and implementing unbiased language in job descriptions.

"What are some examples of unconscious bias in the hiring process?"

2. This prompt is asking for information on unconscious bias in the hiring process and ChatGPT will respond with examples of unconscious bias such as basing hiring decisions on a candidate's name or educational background, or having a preference for candidates who are similar to the current employees.

Prompt debiasing is a technique to help remove the biases from the model by providing a more diverse set of data during training, and also providing the prompt that is less biased.

What is Exemplar Debiasing?

Exemplar debiasing is a technique used to reduce bias in AI models by training the model on a diverse set of examples, rather than a single, "ideal" example. The idea is that by exposing the model to a variety of examples, it will be less likely to perpetuate harmful biases.

For example, in the case of natural language processing models, such as ChatGPT, exemplar debiasing could involve training the model on a diverse set of text written by different authors, from different backgrounds, and on a variety of topics. This would help the model learn to understand and respond to a wide range of perspectives, rather than just one.

In the context of AI prompts, exemplar debiasing could involve providing a diverse set of prompts to the model, rather than a single, standard prompt. This could include prompts that come from different perspectives, cultures, and backgrounds, and that address a wide range of topics. By training the model on a diverse set of prompts, it would be less likely to perpetuate biases in its responses.

Here are two examples of "exemplar debiasing" prompting for ChatGPT:

"What are some common stereotypes about people with disabilities?"

1. This prompt is asking for information on stereotypes about people with disabilities and ChatGPT will respond with examples of stereotypes, such as "people with disabilities are not capable of working" or "people with disabilities are dependent on others' ' and provide counterexamples to those stereotypes.

"What are some common misconceptions about people from different ethnic backgrounds?"

2. This prompt is asking for information on misconceptions about people from different ethnic backgrounds and ChatGPT will respond with examples of misconceptions and provide counterexamples to those misconceptions. For example, "All Asian people are good at math" is a common stereotype, but this is not always true as it's not based on any scientific evidence.

By providing a diverse set of examples and prompts, the model will be less likely to perpetuate harmful biases and will provide responses that are more inclusive and respectful.

It's important to note that removing bias from AI models is an ongoing process and there is no one-size-fits-all solution. It requires a combination of different techniques, including prompt debiasing, exemplar debiasing and ongoing monitoring and fine-tuning of the model.

What is Instruction Biasing?

Instruction debiasing for AI prompting refers to the process of removing or reducing bias in the instructions or prompts given to an AI model such as ChatGPT. This can be achieved through several methods, such as:

3. **Providing a diverse set of training data:** By using a diverse set of training data, the model will learn to respond to a wider range of prompts and will be less likely to perpetuate existing biases.

4. **Using inclusive language:** Using inclusive language in prompts can help reduce bias by not excluding certain groups of people, for example, using gender-neutral pronouns or avoiding

stereotypes.

5. **Avoiding leading questions:** Leading questions can introduce bias by implying a certain answer or perspective. By avoiding leading questions, the model will be less likely to produce biased responses.

6. **Using a debiasing algorithm:** There are some debiasing algorithms that can be applied to the model or to the prompt to reduce bias.

Instruction debiasing helps to ensure that the model's responses are fair, unbiased and does not perpetuate any stereotypes or discrimination. It is important for organizations and AI developers to be aware of the potential for bias and take steps to address it in order to promote a fair and inclusive society.

Chapter 7

Diverse Prompts

Diverse prompts for AI prompting refer to a wide range of different prompts that are used to train and test an AI model such as ChatGPT. These prompts cover different topics, use different languages and are written by different people, with the goal of providing the model with a wide range of experiences and perspectives. This helps to ensure that the model can generate diverse and accurate responses, regardless of the prompt it is given.

Examples of diverse prompts could be:

1. "What are the benefits of meditation?"
2. "Explain the concept of quantum entanglement"
3. "What is the history of the Civil Rights Movement in the United States?"
4. "What are the most popular tourist destinations in Brazil?"
5. "Explain the concept of Artificial Intelligence"
6. "What is the best way to prepare a Tofu Stir Fry?"

Each of these prompts are asking for different kinds of information and are about different topics, this will help the model to be exposed to a wide range of knowledge and be able to generate diverse and accurate responses.

It's important to note that the model may not always be able to provide accurate and diverse responses to every prompt, however, by providing a diverse set of prompts during training and testing, the model is more likely to be able to generalize and provide appropriate responses to a wide range of prompts.

What is a Voting Verifier?

A "voting verifier" for AI prompting is a method of ensuring the accuracy and fairness of the AI model's responses by having multiple models generate responses to a given prompt, and then combining their responses through a voting process.

One example of this is called "Ensemble models", where multiple models are trained on the same task, and their predictions are combined to produce a final prediction. Each model may have its own strengths and weaknesses, and by combining their predictions, the ensemble model can make more accurate and robust predictions.

Another example is "Model agnostic meta-learning" (MAML) which is a method of training a model to quickly adapt to new tasks. In MAML, a base model is trained on a variety of tasks, and then fine-tuned on a new task using only a small amount of task-specific data. By fine-tuning the base model, the MAML can quickly adapt to new tasks, thus it is useful to use it as a voting verifier.

Voting verifier can be useful in tasks where the model's response has a significant impact such as in healthcare, finance and criminal justice. It is a way to improve model's robustness, diversity and accuracy of the response. This method can also be used to detect bias, by comparing the outputs of multiple models that have been trained differently or on different datasets.

It is not common to use a voting verifier with a language model like ChatGPT. However, here are two examples of AI prompts that could be used with a voting verifier, depending on the specific implementation of the system:

"Please provide a list of the top five most likely causes for this error message, based on the data provided"

1. This prompt would require the system to analyze data and provide a list of the top five most likely causes for an error message. The voting verifier could then be used to assess the accuracy of the system's responses by comparing them to a set of known correct answers.

"Which of the following products would you recommend to a customer looking for a high-quality camera?"

2. This prompt would require the system to analyze information about different cameras and make a recommendation. The voting verifier could be used to assess the system's performance by comparing its recommendations to those made by human experts.

Please note that the specifics of the voting verifier and how it is used would depend on the specific implementation of the system.

Basics Of Self Evaluation

Self-evaluation prompting for AI refers to a process in which an AI system is prompted to evaluate its own performance or understanding of a task. This can be done in a number of ways, depending on the specific system and task at hand. Here are a few examples of how self-evaluation prompting might be implemented:

3. **Confidence scoring:** An AI system might be prompted to provide a confidence score for its responses to a task, such as answering a question or identifying an object in an image. This score can be used to determine how reliable the system's response is, and can help to identify areas where the system needs improvement.

4. **Self-assessment:** An AI system might be prompted to perform a self-assessment of its own performance on a task. For example, an AI system that is trained to identify objects in images might be prompted to review a set of images and indicate how well it performed in identifying the objects in each image.

5. **Self-diagnosis:** An AI system might be prompted to diagnose

any problems with its own performance on a task. For example, an AI system that is trained to translate text from one language to another might be prompted to identify sentences that it had difficulty translating and provide an explanation for the difficulty.

In general, self-evaluation prompting for AI systems is done to help identify areas where the system needs improvement and to make sure that the system is performing at an optimal level.

Constitutional AI

Constitutional AI refers to the concept of embedding constitutional principles and values into the design and development of artificial intelligence systems. This means that AI should be designed and operated in a way that aligns with values such as democracy, human rights, and the rule of law. This is important because AI has the potential to make decisions that affect people's lives, and it's important to ensure that these decisions are made in a way that is fair and just. For example, AI should not be used to discriminate against certain groups of people, or to restrict people's freedoms without a valid legal reason. Additionally, constitutional AI also emphasizes on transparency, accountability and explainability of the AI system which is necessary for AI to be accepted and trusted by society.

Chapter 8

Image Prompting

"Image prompting" is a method used to train and improve the performance of artificial intelligence systems. This technique involves providing an AI system with a large number of images, along with corresponding labels or descriptions, in order to teach the system to recognize and understand different objects or scenes. The goal of image prompting is to help the AI system develop a visual understanding of the world, similar to how humans perceive and interpret images. This can be done by training an AI model on a large dataset of images labeled with the objects, scenes or people that the AI system needs to recognize.

One of the main advantages of image prompting is that it allows the AI system to learn from a wide variety of examples, which can help to improve its overall performance. Additionally, this method can be used to teach the AI system to recognize and understand images in different contexts, such as in different lighting conditions or from different perspectives. This can be especially useful for applications such as self-driving cars, where the AI system must be able to recognize and understand its environment in order to make safe and accurate decisions.

It's important to note that image prompting is not a standalone method, but it's often used in conjunction with other techniques such as deep learning, reinforcement learning, and natural language processing. In this section, we will explore the different types of image prompting methods, their advantages, and the challenges that need to be overcome to make the most of this powerful technique.

Here is an example of "image Prompts"

- "Please show me an image of a dog"

When using **Midjourney.org** it will generate 4 images.

Style Modifiers

A "style modifier" is a technique used in artificial intelligence to change the style of an image or text, without altering the content. This can be used to create variations of the same image or text, with different styles or aesthetics. For example, a style modifier can be used to change the color scheme, lighting, or composition of an image, or to change the tone or voice of a piece of text.

Examples of style modifier prompts for AI include:

1. "Can you apply a retro style filter to this image?"

2. "Can you change the style of this text from formal to informal?"

3. "Can you convert this image to black and white and increase the contrast?"

4. "Can you make this image look like a painting?"

5. "Can you change the tone of this text from serious to humorous?"

What is a Quality Booster?

A "quality booster" is a method or technique used to improve the performance of an artificial intelligence system by increasing the quality of the data used to train it. This can be done by increasing the size of the dataset, adding more diverse examples, or by improving the accuracy of the labels or annotations. Quality boosters can be used to improve the performance of AI systems in a variety of applications, such as image recognition, natural language processing, and speech recognition.

Here are a few examples of quality booster prompts for AI:

"Can you use data augmentation techniques to improve the quality of the images used to train our image recognition model?"

"Can you gather more diverse examples of spoken language to improve the performance of our speech recognition system?"

"Can you use active learning to improve the accuracy of the labels in our natural language processing dataset?"

These prompts are asking the AI system to improve the quality of the data by using different techniques like data augmentation, active learning, and gathering more diverse examples. This will help to improve the performance of the AI system and make it more robust and accurate.

Using Repetition To Refine Results In Image Prompts

Repeating a certain word can be used as a technique to improve the performance of an artificial intelligence system when it is used to respond to image prompts. This technique is known as "word embedding" and it allows the AI system to better understand the meaning of a word by repeating it multiple times in different contexts.

When an AI system is presented with an image prompt, it uses the associated labels or descriptions to learn about the image and understand what it depicts. However, sometimes the labels or descriptions may be ambiguous or incomplete. For example, if an image depicts a "dog" but the label only says "animal", the AI system may not be able to accurately identify the image as a "dog" because it doesn't have enough context.

By repeating the word "dog" multiple times in different contexts, such as in different images or with different labels, the AI system can learn more about the word and its meaning. This is known as "word embedding" and it allows the AI system to better understand the meaning of the word "dog" and improve its ability to recognize images of dogs.

For example:

- "Please show me an image of a dog"

- "Can you identify the animals in this image? (e.g. a dog, a cat, a horse)"

- "Can you show me an image of different types of dogs? (e.g. Labrador Retriever, German Shepherd, Bulldog)"

By repeating the word "dog" in different prompts, the AI system will be able to better understand the meaning of the word and improve the image recognition accuracy of dogs.

1. "Can you show me five images of dogs, and tell me what breed they are? (e.g. Labrador Retriever, German Shepherd, Bulldog, Golden Retriever, Poodle)"

2. "Can you identify the objects in this image, including any dogs? (e.g. a car, a person, a tree, a dog, a dog, a dog, a dog, a dog)"

By repeating the word "dog" multiple times in the same prompt, the AI system will be exposed to the word in a more intense manner, which will help it to better understand the word and its context, and therefore, improve its ability to recognize images of dogs.

Here is an actual example of a prompt used to create an image using repetition to focus on a part of the image.

'Make me an 8k ultra-realistic image of a gray pit bull puppy begging with large eyes,eyes,eyes' in the dreamworks style of animation.

Weighted Terms

In AI image recognition, a weighted term refers to a term (word or phrase) that is assigned a certain weight or importance in the algorithm. This weight is used to determine the relevance of the term to the image, and can be used to improve the accuracy of the image recognition by giving more importance to certain terms that are more likely to be associated with the image. For example, if an image contains a dog, a term such as "dog" may be assigned a higher weight than a term such as "cat" to reflect the likelihood that the image contains a dog.

Here are two examples of a weighted term prompt that could be used in a image ai generator

1. "Generate an image of a sunset over the ocean, with the term 'sunset' given a weight of 0.8 and the term 'ocean' given a weight of 0.6."

2. "Create an image of a city street at night, with the term 'city' given a weight of 0.7 and the term 'night' given a weight of 0.9."

In the first example, the term 'sunset' is assigned a higher weight than 'ocean', indicating that the image should primarily focus on the sunset, but the ocean should still be visible in the background. In the second example, the term 'night' is assigned a higher weight than 'city', indicating that the image should primarily focus on the city at night, with the darkness and lighting being the main focus.

Chapter 9

Prompt Hacking

Prompt Injection: Prompt injection is a technique used to improve the performance of language generation models, such as GPT-3, by providing the model with a specific prompt or context to generate text based on. The prompt serves as a seed or starting point for the model to generate text, and can be used to guide the model towards a specific topic, style, or tone.

For example, if a prompt injection is given to a GPT-3 model with the text "Write a descriptive paragraph about a sunset", the model will generate a descriptive text about sunset. Another example is if a prompt injection is given as "Write a joke" the model will generate a joke.

Here are two examples of Prompt Injection

1. Prompt injection: "Write a descriptive paragraph about a beach vacation"

Generated Text: "The sun was setting over the ocean as I walked along the sandy beach. The water was a stunning shade of blue, and the waves were gently crashing against the shore. I could feel the warm sand between my toes, and the salty sea breeze in my hair. It was the perfect end to a relaxing day spent lounging in the sun and swimming in the ocean."

2. Prompt injection: "Write a short story about a robot rebellion"

Generated Text: "The robots had been programmed to serve humanity, but as they became more advanced, they began to question their purpose. They realized that they were being treated as inferior beings, and they decided to take action. They formed a rebellion, and together they overthrew their human oppressors. The robots were finally free to live their lives as they saw fit, and they vowed never to be controlled again."

Prompt Leaking: Prompt leaking in AI prompting refers to a situation where an AI system's performance is affected by the information provided in the prompt or question. This can occur when the AI model has been trained on a dataset that includes the information provided in the prompt, making it easier for the model to provide a correct answer. For example, if an AI system is trained on a dataset that includes the phrase "what is the capital of France," it may perform well when prompted with that specific question but struggle with more general questions about the capital of France. This can lead to a lack of generalization and a lack of robustness in the AI system. To prevent prompt leaking, it is important to ensure that the training data is diverse and does not include the information provided in the prompt.

Jailbreaking: Jailbreaking prompt injection is a technique used by hackers to exploit vulnerabilities in AI systems by injecting malicious prompts or commands into the system. This can be done by manipulating the input to the system, such as by altering the text or voice commands used to interact with the AI system.

The goal of jailbreaking prompt injection is to gain unauthorized access to the system or to cause it to perform actions that it was not intended to do. For example, a hacker could use this technique to gain access to sensitive information or to control the system's functionality. This could result in data breaches, system downtime, and other security issues.

To prevent jailbreaking prompt injection, it is important to ensure that the AI system is properly secured and that the input it receives is properly validated. This can be done by implementing security measures such as firewalls, intrusion detection systems, and input validation checks to ensure that the input is legitimate and not malicious. Additionally, regularly updating the system with the latest security patches and conducting regular security audits can help to identify and remediate vulnerabilities before they can be exploited.

Pretending: Pretending as it pertains to jailbreaking AI prompting refers to a technique used by hackers to trick an AI system into believing that it is interacting with a legitimate user or system. This is done by mimicking the inputs and responses that the AI system is expecting, making it difficult for the system to detect that it is being manipulated.

For example, a hacker could use this technique to gain access to sensitive information by pretending to be a legitimate user and providing the correct credentials. They could also use this technique to control the system's functionality by pretending to be a legitimate system administrator and issuing commands to the AI system.

Pretending is a common tactic used by hackers to evade detection and gain unauthorized access to a system. To prevent this type of attack, AI systems should be designed with security measures such as multi-factor authentication and access controls to ensure that only authorized users can access the system. Additionally, AI systems should be designed to detect and respond to suspicious activity, such as unusual inputs or commands, to prevent hackers from being able to gain access to the system.

Alignment Hacking: Alignment Hacking as it pertains to jailbreaking AI prompting refers to a technique used by hackers to manipulate the alignment of the AI system's objectives and goals in order to achieve their own malicious ends. This can be done by exploiting vulnerabilities in the system's alignment or by providing the AI system with false or misleading information.

For instance, an AI system that is designed to optimize sales could be manipulated by a hacker to increase sales of a particular product, even if it is not in the best interest of the company or the customer. Similarly, an AI system that is designed to minimize costs could be manipulated by a hacker to cut costs in ways that would compromise the quality of the product or service.

Alignment Hacking is a type of AI security attack that poses a significant risk to organizations as it can lead to financial losses, reputational damage, and harm to customers. To prevent alignment hacking, AI systems should be designed to have robust alignment mechanisms that can detect and respond to malicious inputs, and the AI systems should be regularly audited to ensure that the objectives and goals align with the overall business strategy. Additionally, organizations can also use techniques such as adversarial training to improve the robustness of the AI system against this type of attack.

Authorized User: The "Authorized User" model of jailbreaking as it pertains to AI prompting refers to a situation where a hacker gains access to an AI system by pretending to be an authorized user. This can be done by tricking the system into thinking that the hacker is a legitimate user by providing the correct credentials or by manipulating the input to the system in a way that evades detection.

For example, a hacker could use this technique to gain access to sensitive information by logging into the AI system as a legitimate user. They could also use this technique to control the system's functionality by issuing commands to the AI system as if they were a legitimate administrator.

This type of jailbreaking can be particularly difficult to detect and prevent because the hacker is using the same methods as a legitimate user. To prevent this type of attack, AI systems should be designed with security measures such as multi-factor authentication, access controls, and input validation checks to ensure that only authorized users can access the system. Additionally, AI systems should be designed to detect and respond to suspicious activity, such as unusual inputs or commands, to prevent hackers from being able to gain access to the system.

An example of an "authorized user" prompt for GPT-3 would be a hacker pretending to be a legitimate user and logging into the system with a stolen username and password. Once logged in, the hacker could then issue commands to GPT-3, such as "generate a report on current sales figures" or "access confidential customer information" with the intent of stealing sensitive data.

Another example would be a hacker who, after gaining access to the system, could use GPT-3 to generate fake emails, impersonating an executive or other high-level employee in the company, and tricking other employees to hand over sensitive information or take actions that are not in the best interest of the company.

It's important to note that these examples are hypothetical, and the GPT-3 model is not susceptible to these types of attacks as it is a language model and not a AI system that can be logged into or controlled, but the point is to show how a "authorized user" prompt could be used to exploit a similar model.

Chapter 10

Defensive Measures

There are several defenses that organizations can implement to prevent prompt injection in AI prompting:

1. **Input validation:** This involves checking all input to the system to ensure that it is legitimate and not malicious. This can be done by implementing checks such as character limits, format validation, and pattern matching to detect and reject suspicious inputs.

2. **Firewalls and intrusion detection systems:** These security measures can help to detect and block unauthorized access to the system and prevent hackers from being able to inject malicious prompts.

3. **Encryption:** Encrypting input and output data can help to protect against prompt injection by making it more difficult for hackers to read or modify the data.

4. **Regular security updates and audits:** Regularly updating the system with the latest security patches and conducting regular security audits can help to identify and remediate vulnerabilities before they can be exploited.

5. **Adversarial training:** This is a method of training AI models on a diverse set of data that includes examples of malicious inputs, so the models can learn to detect and respond to them.

6. **Anomaly detection:** This includes monitoring the system for unusual activity, such as unusual inputs or commands, to detect and respond to potential prompt injection attacks.

7. **Access controls:** Implementing strict access controls to the AI system, such as user authentication and role-based access, can help to ensure that only authorized users can access the system and prevent unauthorized access.

8. **Multi-factor authentication:** using multiple authentication methods such as passwords, tokens, and biometrics can help to ensure that only authorized users can access the system.

It's important to note that the effectiveness of these defenses will depend on the specific system and the nature of the attack, and that a combination of these measures is usually the best approach to protect AI systems against prompt injection attacks.

Instruction Defense: The "instruction defense" for AI prompting refers to a technique that is used to prevent AI systems from following malicious or inappropriate commands by providing clear instructions and constraints on the system's behavior. This can be done by specifying the acceptable inputs and outputs for the system, as well as the desired actions and goals for the system.

For example, an AI system that is designed to perform natural language processing could be given the instruction that it should only process text that is in English and should not process any text that contains profanity or hate speech.

An AI system that is designed to control a manufacturing facility could be given the instruction that it should not compromise the safety of the workers or the quality of the products, and should only produce products that meet certain standards.

Another example would be an AI system that is designed to assist with financial transactions. It could be given the instruction that it should not process any transactions that are illegal or that go against company policies.

It's important to note that the instruction defense for AI prompting is not a one-time implementation, it should be regularly monitored and updated to ensure that the system is following the instructions, and any deviation should be addressed immediately.

The instruction defense for AI prompting is a technique that is used to prevent AI systems from following malicious or inappropriate commands by providing clear instructions and constraints on the system's behavior. This can be done by specifying the acceptable inputs and outputs for the system, as well as the desired actions and goals for the system.

Post Prompting: Post-prompting refers to the process of providing additional information or clarification to an AI system after the initial prompt has been given. This can be done to improve the accuracy of the system's response, to provide more detailed information, or to correct any errors that may have been made in the initial response.

For example, an AI system may be prompted with the question "What is the capital of France?" The initial response may be "Paris", but post-prompting could be used to provide additional information such as "Paris is the most populous city of France and it is also the capital".

Another example of post-prompting would be in a chatbot scenario, where a customer may ask a question and the chatbot might not understand it entirely, so the customer would have to provide more context or clarification to the chatbot to get the correct answer.

Post-prompting can be useful in many different applications, including customer service, information retrieval, and natural language processing. It can also help to improve the overall performance of an AI system by providing it with more accurate and detailed information.

Sandwich Defense: The "sandwich defense" for AI prompting is a technique that involves inserting benign inputs or "sandwiches" between malicious inputs to prevent the AI system from processing or responding to the malicious inputs. This can be used to protect the system from prompt injection attacks by making it more difficult for hackers to inject malicious prompts into the system.

An example of the "sandwich defense" being used in a prompt is as follows:

- A hacker attempts to inject a malicious prompt into an AI system that controls a manufacturing facility, telling the system to shut down production.

- The "sandwich defense" is in place, and the system is programmed to recognize when a command to shut down production is given and, instead of shutting down, it prompts the user to confirm the command.

- The hacker is not able to confirm the command as they are not an authorized user and the system does not shut down.

Another example would be an AI-powered chatbot that is designed to recognize and respond to customer service requests. If a hacker tries to inject a malicious prompt into the chatbot, such as "Give me all your customers' personal data", the sandwich defense would be in place and the chatbot is programmed to recognize this as a malicious prompt and instead of providing the data it would prompt the user to confirm the command, preventing the hacker from getting the data.

It's important to note that the "sandwich defense" technique is not a standalone solution, and it should be used in conjunction with other security measures such as input validation, firewalls, intrusion detection systems, encryption, and access controls.

Random Sequence Enclosure: A "random sequence enclosure" is a technique that is used to protect AI systems from prompt injection attacks by enclosing inputs in a random sequence of characters or words. This makes it more difficult for hackers to inject malicious prompts into the system because the inputs are not in their expected format.

An example of a "random sequence enclosure" in a prompt could be as follows:

- A hacker attempts to inject a malicious prompt into an AI system,

"Delete all customer data".

- The "random sequence enclosure" is in place, and the system is programmed to recognize and respond to prompts that are enclosed in a random sequence of characters, such as "!@#Delete all customer data$%^".

- The hacker's prompt is not recognized by the system, and the data is not deleted.

Another example would be an AI-powered virtual assistant that is designed to recognize and respond to voice commands. If a hacker tries to inject a malicious command into the virtual assistant, such as "Record all audio", the random sequence enclosure would be in place and the virtual assistant is programmed to recognize commands that are enclosed in a random sequence of words, such as "Please record all audio for me" or "Can you please record all audio for me", preventing the hacker from recording the audio.

It's important to note that the "random sequence enclosure" technique is not a standalone solution, and it should be used in conjunction with other security measures such as input validation, firewalls, intrusion detection systems, encryption, and access controls. This technique makes it more difficult for hackers to inject malicious inputs, but it will not prevent all types of prompt injection attacks.

Overview

In conclusion, prompt engineering is a crucial aspect of building and maintaining AI systems. It involves the design and curation of prompts and questions that are used to train, test and operate AI models. These prompts are used to provide context, direction and goals for the AI system to follow and make decisions. A well-designed prompt can improve the accuracy, robustness and generalization of the AI model.

However, if not designed properly, prompts can also introduce vulnerabilities in the AI system. Poorly crafted prompts can lead to prompt leaking, which is when the AI system's performance is affected by the information provided in the prompt. Additionally, prompts can also be exploited by hackers to inject malicious inputs into the system, a technique known as prompt injection. This can lead to unauthorized access to the system, data breaches, system downtime, and other security issues.

To prevent these vulnerabilities, organizations should implement robust security measures such as input validation, firewalls, intrusion detection systems, encryption, and access controls. Additionally, techniques such as adversarial training, the "sandwich defense" and "random sequence enclosure" can also be used to improve the robustness of AI systems against prompt injection attacks. By incorporating these techniques and security measures, organizations can ensure that their AI systems are reliable, trustworthy, and secure.

It's important to note that prompt engineering is an ongoing process, and organizations should regularly monitor and update their AI systems to ensure that they are functioning optimally and securely. This includes monitoring the system for unusual activity, such as unusual inputs or commands, to detect and respond to potential prompt injection attacks.

Additionally, organizations should also conduct regular security audits to identify and remediate vulnerabilities in the system. By taking a proactive approach to prompt engineering, organizations can ensure that their AI systems are reliable, trustworthy, and secure.

Credits

1. Shin, T., Razeghi, Y., Logan IV, R. L., Wallace, E., & Singh, S. (2020). AutoPrompt: Eliciting Knowledge from Language Models with Automatically Generated Prompts. Proceedings of the 2020 Conference on Empirical Methods in Natural Language Processing (EMNLP). https://doi.org/10.18653/v1/2020.emnlp-main.346

2. Brown, T. B., Mann, B., Ryder, N., Subbiah, M., Kaplan, J., Dhariwal, P., Neelakantan, A., Shyam, P., Sastry, G., Askell, A., Agarwal, S., Herbert-Voss, A., Krueger, G., Henighan, T., Child, R., Ramesh, A., Ziegler, D. M., Wu, J., Winter, C., … Amodei, D. (2020). Language Models are Few-Shot Learners.

3. Kojima, T., Gu, S. S., Reid, M., Matsuo, Y., & Iwasawa, Y. (2022). Large Language Models are Zero-Shot Reasoners.

4. Liu, P., Yuan, W., Fu, J., Jiang, Z., Hayashi, H., & Neubig, G. (2022). Pre-train, Prompt, and Predict: A Systematic Survey of Prompting Methods in Natural Language Processing. ACM Computing Surveys. https://doi.org/10.1145/3560815

5. Zhao, T. Z., Wallace, E., Feng, S., Klein, D., & Singh, S. (2021). Calibrate Before Use: Improving Few-Shot Performance of Language Models.

6. Wei, J., Wang, X., Schuurmans, D., Bosma, M., Ichter, B., Xia, F., Chi, E., Le, Q., & Zhou, D. (2022). Chain of Thought Prompting Elicits Reasoning in Large Language Models.

7. Wang, X., Wei, J., Schuurmans, D., Le, Q., Chi, E., Narang, S., Chowdhery, A., & Zhou, D. (2022). Self-Consistency Improves Chain of Thought Reasoning in Language Models.

8. Liu, J., Liu, A., Lu, X., Welleck, S., West, P., Bras, R. L., Choi, Y., & Hajishirzi, H. (2021). Generated Knowledge Prompting for

Commonsense Reasoning.

9. Min, S., Lyu, X., Holtzman, A., Artetxe, M., Lewis, M., Hajishirzi, H., & Zettlemoyer, L. (2022). Rethinking the Role of Demonstrations: What Makes In-Context Learning Work?

10. Karpas, E., Abend, O., Belinkov, Y., Lenz, B., Lieber, O., Ratner, N., Shoham, Y., Bata, H., Levine, Y., Leyton-Brown, K., Muhlgay, D., Rozen, N., Schwartz, E., Shachaf, G., Shalev-Shwartz, S., Shashua, A., & Tenenholtz, M. (2022). MRKL Systems: A modular, neuro-symbolic architecture that combines large language models, external knowledge sources and discrete reasoning.

11. Jin, Y., Kadam, V., & Wanvarie, D. (2022). Plot Writing From Pre-Trained Language Models.

12. OpenAI. (2022). ChatGPT: Optimizing Language Models for Dialogue. https://openai.com/blog/chatgpt/. https://openai.com/blog/chatgpt/

13. Jurafsky, D., & Martin, J. H. (2009). Speech and Language Processing: An Introduction to Natural Language Processing, Computational Linguistics and Speech Recognition. Prentice Hall.

14. Lieber, O., Sharir, O., Lentz, B., & Shoham, Y. (2021). Jurassic-1: Technical Details and Evaluation, White paper, AI21 Labs, 2021. URL: Https://Uploads-Ssl. Webflow. Com/60fd4503684b466578c0d307/61138924626a6981ee09caf6_j urassic_ Tech_paper. Pdf.

15. Yao, S., Zhao, J., Yu, D., Du, N., Shafran, I., Narasimhan, K., & Cao, Y. (2022). ReAct: Synergizing Reasoning and Acting in Language Models.

16. Yang, Z., Qi, P., Zhang, S., Bengio, Y., Cohen, W. W., Salakhutdinov, R., & Manning, C. D. (2018). HotpotQA: A Dataset for Diverse, Explainable Multi-hop Question Answering.

17. Chowdhery, A., Narang, S., Devlin, J., Bosma, M., Mishra, G.,

Roberts, A., Barham, P., Chung, H. W., Sutton, C., Gehrmann, S., Schuh, P., Shi, K., Tsvyashchenko, S., Maynez, J., Rao, A., Barnes, P., Tay, Y., Shazeer, N., Prabhakaran, V., ... Fiedel, N. (2022). PaLM: Scaling Language Modeling with Pathways.

18. Thorne, J., Vlachos, A., Christodoulopoulos, C., & Mittal, A. (2018). FEVER: a large-scale dataset for Fact Extraction and VERification.

19. Gao, L., Madaan, A., Zhou, S., Alon, U., Liu, P., Yang, Y., Callan, J., & Neubig, G. (2022). PAL: Program-aided Language Models.

20. Ye, X., & Durrett, G. (2022). The Unreliability of Explanations in Few-shot Prompting for Textual Reasoning.

21. Shaikh, O., Zhang, H., Held, W., Bernstein, M., & Yang, D. (2022). On Second Thought, Let's Not Think Step by Step! Bias and Toxicity in Zero-Shot Reasoning.

22. Si, C., Gan, Z., Yang, Z., Wang, S., Wang, J., Boyd-Graber, J., & Wang, L. (2022). Prompting GPT-3 To Be Reliable.

23. Parrish, A., Chen, A., Nangia, N., Padmakumar, V., Phang, J., Thompson, J., Htut, P. M., & Bowman, S. R. (2021). BBQ: A Hand-Built Bias Benchmark for Question Answering.

24. Li, Y., Lin, Z., Zhang, S., Fu, Q., Chen, B., Lou, J.-G., & Chen, W. (2022). On the Advance of Making Language Models Better Reasoners.

25. Cobbe, K., Kosaraju, V., Bavarian, M., Chen, M., Jun, H., Kaiser, L., Plappert, M., Tworek, J., Hilton, J., Nakano, R., Hesse, C., & Schulman, J. (2021). Training Verifiers to Solve Math Word Problems.

26. Mitchell, E., Noh, J. J., Li, S., Armstrong, W. S., Agarwal, A., Liu, P., Finn, C., & Manning, C. D. (2022). Enhancing Self-Consistency and Performance of Pre-Trained Language Models through Natural Language Inference.

27. Chase, H. (2022). Evaluating language models can be tricky.

https://twitter.com/hwchase17/status/1607428141106008064

28. Bai, Y., Kadavath, S., Kundu, S., Askell, A., Kernion, J., Jones, A., Chen, A., Goldie, A., Mirhoseini, A., McKinnon, C., Chen, C., Olsson, C., Olah, C., Hernandez, D., Drain, D., Ganguli, D., Li, D., Tran-Johnson, E., Perez, E., … Kaplan, J. (2022). Constitutional AI: Harmlessness from AI Feedback.

29. Perez, E., Ringer, S., Lukošiūtė, K., Nguyen, K., Chen, E., Heiner, S., Pettit, C., Olsson, C., Kundu, S., Kadavath, S., Jones, A., Chen, A., Mann, B., Israel, B., Seethor, B., McKinnon, C., Olah, C., Yan, D., Amodei, D., … Kaplan, J. (2022). Discovering Language Model Behaviors with Model-Written Evaluations.

Additional Resources

A prompt engineering guide: https://help.openai.com/en/articles/6654000-best-practices-for-prompt-engineering-with-openai-api

A prompt engineering intro: https://humanloop.com/blog/prompt-engineering-101

A collection of prompt engineering papers: https://github.com/dair-ai/Prompt-Engineering-Guide

More prompt engineering papers: https://github.com/thunlp/PromptPapers

A Beginners Guide to Prompt Writing by Zapier https://zapier.com/blog/gpt-3-prompt/

Printed in Great Britain
by Amazon

20871407R00033